SOMETHING MUST BE BROKEN

PRISCILLA BRADFORD

BALBOA.PRESS
A DIVISION OF HAY HOUSE

Copyright © 2020 Priscilla Bradford.

All rights reserved. No part of this book may be used or reproduced by any means, graphic, electronic, or mechanical, including photocopying, recording, taping or by any information storage retrieval system without the written permission of the author except in the case of brief quotations embodied in critical articles and reviews.

Balboa Press books may be ordered through booksellers or by contacting:

Balboa Press
A Division of Hay House
1663 Liberty Drive
Bloomington, IN 47403
www.balboapress.com
844-682-1282

Because of the dynamic nature of the Internet, any web addresses or links contained in this book may have changed since publication and may no longer be valid. The views expressed in this work are solely those of the author and do not necessarily reflect the views of the publisher, and the publisher hereby disclaims any responsibility for them.

The author of this book does not dispense medical advice or prescribe the use of any technique as a form of treatment for physical, emotional, or medical problems without the advice of a physician, either directly or indirectly. The intent of the author is only to offer information of a general nature to help you in your quest for emotional and spiritual well-being. In the event you use any of the information in this book for yourself, which is your constitutional right, the author and the publisher assume no responsibility for your actions.

Any people depicted in stock imagery provided by Getty Images are models, and such images are being used for illustrative purposes only.
Certain stock imagery © Getty Images.

• Amplified Bible, Classic Edition (AMPC)
Copyright © 1954, 1958, 1962, 1964, 1965, 1987 by The Lockman Foundation
• Scripture quotations marked NLT are taken from the Holy Bible, New Living Translation, copyright © 1996, 2004, 2007. Used by permission of Tyndale House Publishers, Inc. Carol Stream, Illinois 60188. All rights reserved. Website

Print information available on the last page.

ISBN: 978-1-9822-5234-2 (sc)
ISBN: 978-1-9822-5235-9 (e)

Balboa Press rev. date: 08/13/2020

Contents

BASIC DEFINITIONS vii
ACKNOWLEDGEMENT ix
INTRODUCTION xi
PRELUDE xiii
PERSONAL NOTE FROM THE AUTHOR xix

WHO IS GOD? 1
RELIGION VS SPIRITUALITY 15
LOVE - TRUE RELIGION 33
PRESSED BEYOND MEASURE 47
SCRIPTURES USED FOR EACH CHAPTER 55
SELF – EVALUATION 57

BASIC DEFINITIONS

UNCONVENTIONAL – "not bound" by or in accordance with convention, *being out of the ordinary.*

BROKEN – having been fractured and damaged and no longer in one piece or in working order; having given up all hope, despairing.

RELIGION (Corporate) – a set of beliefs concerning the cause, nature, and purpose of the universe, especially when considered as the creation of a superhuman agency or ritual observance and often containing a moral code governing the conduct of human affairs. A specific fundamental set of beliefs and practices generally agreed upon by a number of persons or sects, the body of persons adhering to a particular set of beliefs and practices.

"Religion is man-based; therefore you find refuge in someone else's thoughts, words and experiences."

SPIRITUALITY (Individual) – relating to the spirit or soul not to physical nature or matter, intangible, invisible of relating to our source GOD through mediation, sacred text and ethnical development and prayer; experiencing God in a much deeper way. There is a realm He calls us to that is more real. It is spiritual, it is invisible, and it is eternal. That is where the real treasure is.

"Wherever your treasure is, there the desires of your heart will also be." - Matt. 6:21

"All of life is spiritual and therefore all of life's problems are spiritually based and spiritually solved. It comes from within our own self. "Not needing" is a great freedom."

"It is important you understand, you are spirit, since every communication of God with you starts there...Spirit to Spirit."

ACKNOWLEDGEMENT

GOD WHO IS MY EVERYTHING!

Proverbs 27:17 "As iron sharpens iron, so a friend sharpens a friend."

I would like to thank those who sharpened me, by helping me mature physically, and spiritually along my path. Helped me to be the person I am today "A better me." I will always love you with no conditions!

There are many who have touched my life, however I would like to give a special acknowledgment to Renetha Macklin and Dr. Claudette Anderson Copeland.

(My siblings)

Julie, Chico, Ruth, Grace, Michael and Peter

Mary Johnson, Michelle Hayes and Kim Pittman (surrogate)

(My in laws)

Julinda Boggs (mother), Christine Crowder (sister) and Reginald Boggs (brother)

(My children)

Shaheed, Jesse Jonathan, Aaliyah, Erica

Camille Marbury, and Debra Spann (surrogate)

Isaiah, Priscilla, Adam, Jeramiah, Sienna (grandchildren)

Isiah Leos (surrogate)

To my incredible gifted husband - James you are my safe place, my joy and laughter, friend, lover, my Clark Kent at times, but always my SUPERMAN!

Like to give a shout out to my Kenya Family

Pastor Silas, Lady Christine, Peter, Karen and little Priscilla

INTRODUCTION

*"Not everything that is faced can be changed,
but nothing can be changed until it's faced."
- James Baldwin*

Most religions believe in God, while some believe in a Higher Power, Source, Mother Nature, and Universe. They started out with God it became man-made (ego base) it became broken, leaving those that believe remaining broken as well. No freedom, no peace and no real love.

The idea that religion and spirituality are fundamentally connected and many believe they are the same....they are not. There are real DIFFERENCES between the two and I am going to attempt to show the DIFFERENCES.

Religion is one belief system, a community, one united body, and it creates outreach programs for those in need. However, at times it can create, self-interest, greed, one divided body among believers, and strife. Therefore, coming to my conclusion **"Something must be broken."**

Spirituality creates one with God, love with no conditions, limitless and endless relationship with your Creator. It is open to everyone, and it's promises are not hidden. It Creates peace of mind and a life of freedom. **Nothing missing, nothing broken**, *just wholeness and healing. No judgment, no conditions, no shame, just true Spirituality.*

PRELUDE

By James A. Bradford

Religion has boundaries. You can do this but can't do that. You can go here, but not there. You can dress or look like this, but you can't dress or look like that....

Spirituality has no boundaries. There are no boundaries in thought. Think about if you were physically incarcerated, your mind has the freedom to go or to think whatever, which is outside the boundaries of being incarcerated.

God says true religion or the book of James says "True religion is to help the widows, the fatherless...people or folks in need. God says, "True religion has a lot to do with your behavior; something that has to do with your heart, a Samaritan, a relief effort to support, and to help a hurting world. But during Jesus time the Jews were bias towards people or folk that were born half Jew and half Gentile, who were called Samaritans which were not acceptable at that time.

The Book of Luke 10:33 talks about the Good Samaritan...the outcast, that Jesus was proud of and proclaimed hero.

Spirituality has much more to do with behavior. Like accountability, caring, which Godliness is contentment in a bias environment; Jesus points out...The Good Samaritan... God offers us no limits, no boundaries, no lies. Let me explain (lies) let's call it misdirection...the act or process of directing someone to the wrong place or in the wrong direction. Magicians do this all the time when performing a trick. They get you to look one way, while the trick is being evolved another way. Example: Let say I got you believing if you steal an ink pen or sneaking candy and popcorn into a movie theater is not of God or Godly; but to tell a religious believer that God will bless them more if they put in more money into to church or just give more money, or use credit cards and put your home bills on a back burner, cause God said, "you would get a special blessing giving $1000 tonight", is honorable? What kind of thinking is this?

Luke 10:34, 37 (AMPC) "And went to him and dressed his wounds, pouring on (them) oil and wine. Then he set him on his own beast and brought him to an inn and took care of him. (35) And the next day he took out two denarii (two days wages) and gave (them) to the innkeeper, saying, Take care of him; and whatever more you spend, I (myself) will repay you when I return. (36) Which of these three do you think proved himself a neighbor to him who fell among the robbers? (37) He answered the one who showed pity and mercy to him. And Jesus said to him, "Go and do likewise."

God defines you, God validates you. Spirituality is living… life is life. You can crawl in a closet or live in the forest or be the greatest news on the internet, but the author's goal is to make you aware that spirituality and religion has two totally different conclusions.

Religion has boundaries – A god Spirituality is unlimited – God Almighty

The author Priscilla is going to have you fact check your belief, your thoughts, your doubts. Spirituality will make you look into your soul, your eyes, your truth and decide is it a lie (misdirection) or is it the Truth the genesis of where you are, why or when did it start, why or where did it come from.

Don't misunderstand me, I'm not getting you to choose between religion and spirituality, but I'm encouraging you that (I quote) *"Religion is the means, not the end. It is the map, not the territory. It is the cover not the book." David Hawkins*

Judgment, punishment, conflict, brutality, violence, and prejudice. **Ralph Waldo Emerson said, *"Your actions speak so loudly, I can't hear what you are saying."***

Folks have you ever read the Book of Judges? (The Old Testament) The Old Testament in my opinion was to create a level playing field, for the <u>Haves</u> and the <u>Have Nots.</u> Because images can shape your behavior...when you see fashion or new styles, or new experiences and challenges and epiphanies...wonders, your opinion and emotions becomes so curious. Then your beliefs become one of the facts that are based on your religious beliefs; your language, and conflict with your judgment.

Your limits are cast out before all can see your judgment. The boundaries you have chosen for you. You have to ask yourself, because of religion, How far will you go? Religion is about boundaries...the author is not suggesting that Spirituality has no boundaries, there are no limits, or that Spirituality is or is not influenced by religion. But as you read more of the content of this book, a person that is Spiritual acknowledges God above religion and a religious person acknowledges their beliefs about who or what God is, but God is God, not an ideology.

God is supreme, God is omnipotent, and God is omnipresent. God is judge, God is all knowledge. God is the God of gods, King of kings and Lord of lords. We are made in God's image, God's not made in our image. God is a celestial being; God is not an old white man with a long white beard sitting on a throne, in heaven. God is the soul of what gives human beings life, the spirit of life inside us that gives us life.

To a non-believer, folks being an atheist or (someone who believes there is no God), or don't believe in hell because that is logical to them. One thing that the author will point out that is logical and what is logical to the non-believer is you have <u>life</u> in you. And all your decision making as you live, comes from that <u>life</u> you have. Where you got that <u>life</u> that is in you…is the question. Because all birth or attempted birth is not successful. But there is <u>only</u> <u>one</u> explanation that pass the smell test for <u>life</u>, and that is… "IT'S ALIVE!!! No one argues the living. If you're alive or dead you know it!

Spirituality argues life after death; spirituality argues boundaries with no limits. Folks that don't believe in religion, or church or the bible…I get that…I also was against these, apparent superficial ideas. As Priscilla goes into the superficial difference between Spirituality and Religion…you might be pleasantly surprised…that Spirituality goes far beyond religion and that without being aware, you may discover that you are more Spiritual than you think, and Jesus & God is not about religion they are about Spirituality. The…"RU-BRIC" (the truth we walk by) so to speak of what you feel or think.

There are lots of folks who now say I'm Spiritual not religious…I get that I was like that at one time. People don't validate who we are…God defines who we are. But let me ask you…reader…if you had just <u>one</u> choice to be <u>right</u> or to be <u>kind</u>, which would you choose? I would say, if you are spiritual you would choose kind. I think so, because we are made in the image of <u>God</u>…our spirituality, our life, who we are…is defined by God.

Not religion, not people, not our circumstances. Our circumstances don't define us; it just reveals the choices we made at the time. Absconding – leave hurried and secretly, typically to avoid detainment or arrest. This behavior today is typical of folks to ignore or to hide from, people that are religious, because of judgment, or religious principles. Who wants to be judged all the time? Especially when no one is perfect! Everybody has done something (Checkered) or bad. Even people who call themselves saints, does not always act saintly. But we as people are always human…you can believe that. Human beings are naturally inquisitive, so gossipy and judgment is always on the table.

To get being spiritual all tangled with religion or religious practices is just plain wrong. They are different. The author is going to attempt to show you the difference and…how important it is for you to know the difference.

Remember Ralph Waldo Emerson's said, "Your action is so loudly, I can't hear what you are saying." God said, "Learn of me for my yoke is easy, and my burdens are light." Your unbelief in religion or God is just one of the things on God's plate, believe me, God can handle what you are dealing with.

PERSONAL NOTE FROM THE AUTHOR
"MY TRUTH"

"God approved of you, before anyone else ever got a chance to disapprove!"

"A friend that understand your tears, is more valuable than a lot of friends that only know your smile."

Parables = Word Pictures – Jesus loved to speak in *"word pictures."* I too will attempt to give you "Word Pictures;" explanations of things, events that you can understand, making it as simple as possible. That you will see what I see, understand what I understand, and experience what I have experienced...My Truth!

Everyone that hears the Word of God doesn't necessarily understand His Word. Most people accept God because of how they felt inside and how He touched their heart, but your understanding of who God is came later. However, just because you became a believer at that moment, doesn't necessarily mean you are not still broken inside. You can be saved but still bound. It doesn't make you faithless; it means you need to trust God with the healing process of your heart; with the issues of your heart. Your physical body performs better with a healed soul/heart. A lot of sickness and diseases are exhibit because of a heart that is broken, a heart that is bound, filled of hatred, bitterness, un-forgiveness and revenge. When you operate in this way you doubt that God desires to heal you. You know He can you just don't think He would do it for you. You don't believe He values you when you compare His love with past relationships and their definition of love. They didn't think you were worth the trouble, they didn't value you, they walked away when you didn't perform to their expectations, so you think God's love is the same, but it's not. In Japan broken objects are often repaired (not replaced) with Gold. The flaw is seen as a unique piece of the objects history, which adds to its beauty. When you change the way you look at things, the things you look at change. His love has no conditions attached. His Word starts and ends with relationship and love (GOD). All of life issues begin in the heart (emotions, experiences).

Proverbs 4:23 (NLT) says, "Guard your heart above ALL else, for it DETERMINES the course of your life." When you don't guard your heart, you operate with a foolish heart that can destroy you. *Proverbs 5:21-23 (NLT) "For the Lord sees clearly what a man does examining every path he takes. (22) An evil man is held captive by his own sins; they are ropes that catch and hold him. (23) He will die for lack of self-control; he will be lost because of his great foolishness.* Issues from the heart blind your perception of life, people's intent, situations you face when you can't let go and let God heal you; you won't let Him guide you down your path and you decide you're in charge of your own life. It feels better to hold onto the pain, building a wall between you and everyone, including God, which obstructs your vision of knowing God and His kind of love for you. He created you out of love. He put EVERYTHING inside you to help you navigate this physical world out of love. He put a treasure chest within you, a place for you to commune with Him out of love. It begins with the renewing of your mind, your thoughts, how you see and feel about you and then everything else will change. Once the Word gets inside you, it will perform in due time. Understanding truth always brings change, and requires an open non-judgmental heart. Your purpose is to love, empower, encourage, touch those around you, so you can help each person along their pathway and God will do the rest. True freedom comes when you see yourself as a caretaker and not an owner of people's lives, their problems, their issues and their choices.

For years I struggled within myself, trying to find this "peace that surpasses all understanding." This life that promised "joy unspeakable and full of glory". A life of abundance, blessings and real love. For years I thought I knew God but all I found was struggles, pain, frustration, depression, disappointments and conditional love. Finally, I realized what I knew about God came from others belief system and it just wasn't working for me. I had nowhere else to go (so I thought), but when one night in my despair, and my hopelessness… I cried out to God "If you are real, I want to KNOW YOU!" And at that moment I found myself laying in the Presence of God and I became engulfed in His love, my mask came off and my walls crumbled in a moment of transparency and vulnerability. God answered me, He said, "Forget all you think you know about me and I will show you WHO I AM." More importantly I realized if God has a Presence, He could be known, experienced and touched…and He touched me that night and I will never forget it.

It was at that moment I opened my heart, and cleared my mind and my journey changed course. God appointing people to come at each phase of my journey. He brought extraordinary books that broaden my understanding of Him which changed me from the inside out. But it happened when I decided to invite Him in to guide me, and to teach me, with no one else's understanding. It wasn't easy for me to let go of everything I was told or thought I knew, but I put my life, my whole being in God's hands.

I found out God is more than one dimensional, more than a one way thinking and operating God. He showed me He always loved with no conditions. He has always been a part of my life, even when I didn't acknowledge Him. He was always connected to me. He never left me, He was always there. Today I can say, I love God and I know who I am in Him. I now know what it means to have peace that surpasses understanding and joy unspeakable and full of His Glory. The moments I spend with Him is priceless, it brings freedom and peace to my heart and my soul. I see His mysteries, I understand them and it has nothing to do with religion, or being religious. It's all spiritual. Don't misunderstand me; this world needs churches and ministries, because that's where the majority of unbelievers turn to when they desire to know God and look for answers to deal with their heart issues.

So, this book is not an indictment on religion, I'm not saying religion is wrong, I'm saying, how do you feel about it? The objective of this book is to provide the means to lift off from a world of struggle, pain, and frustration and sail into a vast universe of possibilities. It's about self-examination, self –evaluation and self-realization; this book is about you. About how you see your life (where did that belief system come from), how you feel about yourself (what were you taught about self-love) and how you see God (do you really know Him) Your life isn't about religion, but living a life of spirituality, a life of opportunity and a life of experiencing God for yourself. Staying connected to HIM and making sure your connection doesn't become corroded.

God is there to anyone that seeks Him no matter where, in prison, in a car, a park, a church, your job, or in the midst of trouble, abuse, trauma and loss of a loved one, or in your brokenness. He is there waiting for you to invite Him to help, heal and protect.

Jesus said, "You will KNOW the TRUTH and the TRUTH will SET you FREE!"

Ask yourself…Why am I still bound! You have been hearing and reading the Word of God for years, so why aren't you free? What is stopping you from becoming free?

I challenge you to evaluate your belief, not on someone else's thoughts about it or others interpretation of who God is or what God needs. For God needs NOTHING, He lacks NOTHING, He is PERFECT, POWERFUL, and is COMPLETE. Knowing God, having a relationship with God is for your benefit. God desires to help you get where you desire to be...FREE and PEACEFUL, and to have joy, love, and to live life on purpose not just existing.

Take off all these expectations that others have put on you. God says love me, love yourself, and love your neighbor that's it!!!! That is true religion. Nothing else matters. If you can just do that, you will find true freedom and a life without judgment, without condemnation, without shame and without guilt. Life is just life. God created EVERYTHING for you to enjoy! ***1 Tim 4:4 (NLT) "Since everything God created is good, we should not REJECT any of it, but receive it with thanks!"*** Why continue to put restrictions on your life, when you love God, God becomes your guide and He NEVER steers you wrong! He is right there with you, experiencing everything you do, because He literally lives inside you. You are the breath of GOD! He says the Kingdom of God is within you!

As you read the following chapters, you will feel the urge to judge me, my words, and my thoughts, I hope you won't. My desire for you is to open your mind, your heart and let God guide you, Spirit to spirit. Take pause and take a hard look at where your life is. What I am writing is my experiences, my truth; this is what I have experienced and came to my conclusion for me. I had no peace, love, joy, forgiveness and no freedom, saved, yet broken, so I needed to examine why. My journey brought me here, this is about me. I am just sharing how I have come to where I find myself today...totally free and making a better version of myself every day; living God conscience, not sin conscience.

Not living my life the way I do because it is required of me, but because I desire to. I find myself loving without conditions.

When I began practicing unconditional love, it was hard and uncomfortable. As a human being I was taught by others behavior, there is always conditions to sharing your love. But as I continue to practice and understand love without getting anything in return it became easier each day. Pain and expectations disappeared. I realize how you love is learned behavior, so I needed to <u>relearn</u> what real love was. I had to <u>renew</u> my thoughts, and my mind to line up with God's kind of love. It has brought peace and freedom to my spirit, no judging others for who they are, just love them. It has helped me to do ME and in doing ME I have learned to do GOD, which brings real freedom, real peace and real love.

I don't believe God brought you to this book to create confusion, but there is something you have been asking God to do for you. Sometimes God doesn't answer the way you think He should, the answer comes the way He thinks it should. So here you are getting ready to change your life, you're thinking, and your heart if you just let go and let God do it. God can restore what is broken and change it into something amazing. All you need is FAITH and TRUTH!

Your judgment keeps you from joy and your expectations on others make you unhappy. Please leave the judgment and offense at the door and read this book with great expectation of change for your life!

If you're not truly free, if you're not living a life of peace and joy, no secrets, no transparency; you're not true to yourself, then there must be a change. God desires for you to have all you desire in life, no limits, and no boundaries. Everything you think or ask is your, if you just believe it! You will find change, freedom and love if you choose it this day! That decision has ALWAYS been yours!

WHO IS GOD?

"I will not let anyone walk through my mind with their dirty feet."

- Gandhi

To the Corporate body, the church folk, you will find words that flow from their lips as they quote every scripture they memorized in Sunday school, it will be familiar descriptions and even profound... He is the Almighty...The Creator of the Universe...King of kings and Lord of lords.

To the scientist who have studied God...He is Supreme Being...He is Source...To Albert Eisenstein He was "A superior reasoning power, revealed in the incomprehensible universe." Can it get any deeper than that!

To Hollywood He is Morgan Freedman in "Bruce Almighty" or George Burns in "Oh God!"

To the theologian, He is Jehovah Jirah, God our Provider, Jehovah Shalom, God our peace, Jehovah Nissi, God our banner. He is all knowing, all wisdom, everywhere at one time. I can go on and on and on... however, my question is, "Who is God to you?"

This reminds me of a story I read about. ***It is a story of a group of blind men who have never come across an elephant before and who learned what the elephant is like by touching*** *it. The blind man creates his own version of reality from that limited experience.*

First blind man touches the elephant's side and exclaims "He is exactly like a wall." Second man touches the tusk and he said, "My brother you are mistaken, he is round and smooth and sharp. He is more like a spear than anything else". The third man took a hold of his trunk. He said, "you are both wrong, he is like a snake." The fourth one reaches out and grabs his leg. He says, "Oh how blind you are, he is round and tall like a tree." The fifth man was very tall and took a hold of his ear. He says, "he is exactly like a huge fan." The sixth man seized his tail and said, "Oh foolish fellows, he is like a rope."

The blind men and the elephant is an ancient parable used today as a warning for people that promote absolute truth or exclusive religious claims. We are just as foolish and blind when we allow other people's limited perceptions, and life experiences lead to overreaching misinterpretations of who God is.

God is defined by 1) What you have been taught or told about Who God is 2) Your personal experiences with God and 3) Who God really is. In different stages of your life God becomes what you need Him to be. As a child I had a different perception of who God was.

I knew or was taught that God existed. Never really was acquainted with Him, just knew He lived in heaven, you know kid stuff. My dad was an alcoholic and people used to come and try to get my parents to their church, but when that didn't happen they would come and pick us up and take us. They would take us to Vacation Bible School (which was like a summer school that consisted of games, bible stories, snacks), in hopes that my parents would soon follow.

My dad was loving and kind when he was sober, however when he was drunk he became a different person, he was uncaring, loud, mean, and abusive. He was a monster! My mom became his punching bag and we became colleterial damage. He was verbally and physically abusive to us all. He was always looking for a fight when that alcohol took ahold of him.

I was told that he would leave the house and stay away 2 to 3 days on a drinking binge. He would go to this empty lot with his pals and they would make a fire and stay there until the booze was gone, then they would make their way back to their homes. One of his drinking binges, when the booze ran out my dad was on his way home, when he heard music playing from a distance. I'm sure he thought this must be a party going on, so in his drunken state he proceeded to follow the music and singing.

The music and singing was coming from a small church, which my dad didn't even realize. He opened the door and kept walking towards the person playing the piano. Once he got to the front of the church the ministers surrounded him and began to pray for him. After a few hours he stood up and he was sober. My mom and older sister were getting ready to go out to look for my him, when out of nowhere the door opened and as quite as a mouse there my dad stood. My mom asked him where he was and he said church and he turned and went to bed.

A few days passed and my dad decided to disappear again and the same thing happened, he ended up at the church after the booze ran out, and again they prayed for him and he was sober. But this time before he can turn and leave the Pastor took some information from him; his name, where he lived. A couple of days later they showed up at our door, they were having a revival and wanted them to attend, so they did. My mom and my dad gave their hearts to Jesus and were saved, I was six years old.

When my parents got saved and began their Christian journey they entered a new phase that was foreign to me. When I say foreign I mean everything that was familiar had changed in our household. I was taught things about doctrine, belief systems and tradition with a trusting eye and trusting ear. Most people grow up believing in God and would pray to Him in time of need, but when you get involved in religion, it takes you to a whole new level of who God is.

To know God means to have an understanding of His character and His ways, the principles by which He operates. Sadly many spend a lifetime only knowing about Him.

You only know people to the degree you know their character, not just their personalities. When you don't take time to be with Him and know God's character, you'll always have and give a one sided and unclear view of Him.

CHRISTIANITY *is not a voice in the wilderness, but a life in the world. It is not an idea in the air but feet on the ground, going God's way. It is not a novelty to be kept under glass, but a hardy plant to bear twelve months of fruits in all kinds of weather. Fidelity to duty is its root and branch. Nothing we can say to the Lord, no calling Him by great or dear names, can take the place of the plain doing of His will. We may cry out about the beauty of eating bread with Him in His Kingdom, but it is wasted breath and rootless hope, unless we plow the plant in His kingdom here and now. To remember Him at His table and to forget Him at ours is to have invested in bad securities. There is no substitute for plain, every-day goodness. - Babcock*

When you get involved in a religion, you don't only get taught who God is, but you also get people's ideas and opinion of God. Your belief begins when someone else tells you it's true and this is how it is. You don't question it because those teaching have been a part of their environment for years, of course they know what they are talking about.

It's funny even at a young age I always questioned some church doctrines, rituals, etc. I felt it had nothing to do with my relationship with God. It was a battle I had inside and would always dismiss it and believe the Preacher. He couldn't be wrong, it was the prayers of the believers, that brought my father to an altar my dad was transformed. It was a miracle; this had to be the way to God. So, I believed everything they taught me, without question, irrespective of the unsettling I felt inside me.

The older I got the more my soul became restless. Even in seminary I would challenge the instructors when they would teach church doctrine as Bible. I was so frustrated with God, unfulfilled in my life I thought He was unfair to have created all of this and I could not participate in it. He was the God of rules and regulations. The God of condemnation. All I was living for was the second coming, the rapture, everything else was sin. It was sin to take pride in myself, my appearance, and my body. Even though God said, when He created me, I was GOOD! He created the earth for my enjoyment, for me to reproduce and be fruitful. Yet if I did not live the way I was told, I was on my way to HELL! God was sitting way up in heaven waiting for me to screw up, so He could punish me. He loved me, but there were conditions to His love. A lot of what I did or didn't do, became the condition for God's love; living a life of condemnation, shame and guilt. So I found myself serving God out of obligation and not real LOVE! I had only one perception of who God was, I never realized God was much more than a harsh and unforgiving God. God just didn't make sense to me, because my understanding was based on someone else's interpretation of Him. I would dismiss God when He would try to help me understand who He really was. I remained saved, but still broken!

I was trying to conform myself to a God that I was taught was a conventional God, and guess what, I am not the only one, there is still people living that way. Do you know there are 42,000 versions of Christianity? Don't we all believe in the same God? Jesus Christ was God wrapped in humanity and you are created in His image and likeness. ***Colossians 1:15 (NLT) "Christ is the visible image of the invisible God. He existed before anything was created and is supreme over all creation."***

God has no visible body here in this physical world and God is only a part of religion. Everything you do in life is based on your knowledge, perceptions, beliefs and experiences of God. You will find your thoughts of God will be different, depending on your understanding of Him and who you talk to. No one person sees God the same. Each person has their own ideas of who God is. To some God is a man, woman, nature, earth, Source, Spirit, Jesus, Allah, Yahweh, Elohim, Father, Mother, Universe. He is also the God of Judgment, and condemnation, or the God of love and forgiveness, and still to some the God of Power, prosperity and protection, and there are those who have no idea at all. God has many attributes that have been given to Him.

Unfortunately, religion has created a sin conscience message - living your whole life by rules and regulations without question. Serving God out of obligation, waiting to be judged to hell or waiting to be punished with every move you make, which forms a wall that keeps you from knowing God. In place of a God Conscience message, understanding God is not difficult to find, He is impossible to avoid, He is in plain sight! He is everywhere and in everyone.

I have observed that religious people can be a dangerous bunch; I know I use to be one. You become the 21st Century Pharisees, Sadducees and Scribes; indulging in yourself, your ego, and no love for God's creation…humanity. You forget the most important part of being as God, is to love God, love yourself, and love your neighbor. The 10 Commandments are all about relationship and love? The 10 Commitments/Commandments – **Love God** - you shall have no other gods but me. You shall not misuse my name. **Love Yourself** - You shall remember the Sabbath (rest), Respect your father and mother, you must not steal, you must not commit murder, you must not commit adultery. **Love Your Neighbor** – You must not give false evidence against your neighbor, you must not be envious of your neighbor's goods. You shall not be envious of his house, wife, nor anything that belongs to your neighbor. If you operate in love, the commandments become your commitment to God. Loving God, loving yourself and loving your neighbor.

Outward appearance has no place in God, once you go within yourself God will show you who He is and when the inside begins to heal the outside will change. You become Spiritual, Not Religious. God is a Spirit and those that worship, and love Him, must worship, and love Him in Spirit…Spirit to spirit…that's the real way to know Him. I can memorize and quote scriptures from the Bible, but if I never live or experience those scriptures for myself, then all I have are words with no experience.

EVERY Religion is based on their own interpretation of God. His requirements of how you should pray, look, act, eat, drink, believe, events you should participate in, entertainment, everything outward and nothing inward. Versus are taken from the Bible and religion/churches are built around those scriptures. You justify your indictment of non-believers with verses that were never intended to be used that way. You judge others because they don't believe what you believe. And don't get me started on the money part of the church. Using God to get what you want or need for your own lifestyle. Living life this way is a dangerous place to be in. You become judgmental, self-righteous, defenders of the gospel instead of lovers of the gospel and lovers of the people. You are so quick to condemn people and to separate yourself from them. You think you're better than those that don't believe, because you say you have God in your life and you know God. You're not better than anyone, your only better than you use to be because of God's mercy and grace.

Those that live a godly life and have a relationship with God do not look any different from anyone else. They don't wear special clothes, jewelry, to let anyone know they are godly and have a special relationship with God. It's not what you wear it's how you live. Behavior (how you live) is a better indicator of what you believe than words. Your behavior will always betray your words.

"It is not for you to judge the journey of another soul. It is for you to decide who You are, not who another has been or has failed to be."

Many people believe in God, and there are those that deny there is a God, but all creation even those that deny God can feel and know He exist. Again I ask you, who is God? He is your intuition, not what you think you know, but what you feel inside yourself! God is created through your own human values, and your moral compass yet He is still more than that. He is at the center of your being. You can't place Him in a box where each religion tries so hard to do. He is all of Creation! There is more to God than you will ever experience.

When you attach rules, traditions and conditions to having a relationship with God, you encourage a one-sided relationship, and therefore you don't find any change in yourself. If He loves you the way you understand love to be, and depending on your thoughts about love, especially if it comes from a place of pain, unhappiness and conditions you will not understand His love. You find yourself serving God out of obligation, which makes it easier for you, because of course you know how to do that, you have been doing that your whole life. Everything in life has conditions, why not God's love. You don't try to understand God; you'd rather take someone else's teaching about who He is. In doing so, you take no responsibility when things don't work out for you; you have the teacher or leader to blame. "*Progress is impossible without change, and those who cannot change their mind cannot change anything." George Bernard Shaw* You cannot change the past you can only live this present moment.

It is vital to know Who God is, so you will understand who you are. God did not discover you, He created you. He just didn't create you, but He created you in His image and likeness. What does that mean? It definitely does not mean our physical bodies look like God, although He can adapt to whatever form He chooses for a particular purpose. ***Genesis 18:1 (NLT) "The Lord appeared again to Abraham near the oak grove..."*** It does mean that your essence, your spirit is the same as God. You are composed of the same stuff, with all the same properties and abilities including the ability to create physical reality out of thin air, if you believe it. When you see me, you should see God...His likeness, same character and same power. When you know for sure who God is, you will know yourself, because God is in you and you are in Him...covenant partners...connected!! You live it, because you experienced Him in everything that you do.

Christ said, there is NO CONDEMNATION who is in Christ Jesus. When you understand the principals of Christ, His teachings, LIVING His examples, you begin to understanding the Power that you have within, no condemnation, no shame and no guilt in your life. You realize life is just life; array of experiences that eventually will bring you to God, if you remain open to Him. Every experience in life is the path to getting to know God and finding who you really are in Him. So, don't condemn your past, thank God for it! This place of knowing is a place of intense and incredible gratitude, thanking Him in advance. To be thankful for your past experiences and your present moments! Everything you have experienced in life, good or bad was designed to steer you back to God. Stop living life with regrets; it has brought you here, this moment for change...freedom...truth!

Jesus said you would do greater things than He did. How powerful a statement is that? Instead of hearing power, self-reliance, and dependence on God from the teachings, you hear unworthiness, imperfection, conditional God, Hell and the devil. You can't understand why you are still in the state of stress, poverty, pain, and bondage. YOU HEAR NO POWER... YOU CAN'T DO IT WITHOUT ME (Religion) TELLING YOU WHERE TO GO, HOW TO GO, WHEN TO GO, AND WHY TO GO. Jesus had the disciples three years and before He died, the disciples were teaching, praying and healing folks. They scattered to preach the good news, not the sad news, but the good news, that you too are POWERFUL and can do ALL that Christ has done. They taught, encouraged, and established disciples to keep the gospel alive and moved on.

Jesus didn't tell you to build great cathedrals, hold on to your congregation, and make sure they only rely on you. NO, He wanted EVERYONE to know the Kingdom of Heaven was in each and every one of you, you are the church, not the building, you are the living, breathing church and you are to live it so others could be saved. Living it, experiencing it, not hoarding it, not exclusive, but inclusive, it is for EVERYONE. He died for EVERYONE. It is your purpose to make that so; Truth, Spirituality, not religion, rules, selfishness, hidden agendas; living the good news, the unadulterated Word of God. Unconditional love means just that without conditions, without profit, without hidden agendas, without self-indulgence.

Your mind creates a FALSE GOD according to your belief system and thoughts. *"Falsehood is not the opposite of Truth, but merely its absence, just as darkness is not the opposite of light, but merely represents the lack of it." David Hawkins* You have created a God who demands worship and sacrifice, however God is complete, perfect, and lacks nothing and does not require anything, but for you to realize who <u>you are</u> in Him. You have created God in your image and likeness, so He can fit into your lifestyle, your perceptions, and your way of thinking. James wrote "Embrace trials, hardships, temptations, with JOY,

WHY? because in doing so, it gives you an opportunity to put a mirror to yourself, so you can evaluate yourself, heal yourself, overcome and become complete, and perfect lacking nothing." Your worship, and praise comes from a grateful heart, a heart that realizes how AWESOME your Creator, your Source, God is and His love for you. The benefit is yours not God. God knows when you finally get it, you become free of others perception, and ideas of Him. He is always present in your life whether you acknowledge Him or not.

"Who is God? A question I asked in a time of struggles, confusion and loneliness. In my years of religious service, (ministry) I had many days of financial, spiritual and emotional struggles. My heart held more questions than answers. I saw myself running away from God, instead of to Him. Many people have this notion that those who work in ministry have it made...not so! Just because you work in ministry doesn't mean you have no struggles, and have an intimate relationship with God; some fake it until they make it! When you're depressed, lonely and sadness takes a hold of your life, it's hard to love anyone, even God. When I found myself in this state, which was more times than not; all I wanted was to die. My back against the wall, I was going to church and nothing changing. Hearing the same old messages that just reinforced my feeling; no message of Hope, Power, or Encouragement! I felt so defeated, and suffocating in the life I was living, so I tried experience stuff outside my church boundaries, drinking, partying and working day and night. I wasn't there for my children, because I was chasing the "American Dream," trying to make this pain go away. I didn't realize all I needed to do was go inside myself so God could heal me. The "American Dream" was not the answer to the unfulfilled life I was experiencing. I needed God, but in my state of mind, I felt God didn't want any part of me, or loved me. I was not the person He wanted representing Him. I was alone and nowhere to turn. But God is so faithful He stepped in when I thought it was over for me. He loved me so much that He wasn't going to allow me to drown without a life saver to hold

onto. So I held on tight, opened my heart and trusted Him to bring the answers that I needed, and He did.

He lead me to books about meditation, how to quiet my mind. At first, I fought God, because to mediate or learn to quiet your mind was considered "NEW AGE"! Why would God send me in that direction? Ignorance is not bliss…knowledge and experience is! It was hard at first to shut down my mind to the outside world, my ideas and thoughts; learning to come to God without asking for anything, but waiting on Him to fill me up with His presence. This technique worked for me the best. I would close my eyes, I pictured God as my Father sitting on a bench and I was a child with my head on His lap as He stroked my hair and we simply connected.

I began to know God, develop a relationship with Him, my picture of God changed and so did my knowledge of Him. This knowledge has brought peace to my soul, excitement to my spirit. The more time I spend with Him, I become overwhelmed, my heart feels like it could burst, tears flood my face, but I don't care, I am in the midst of pure love, and desire to stay right there wrapped up in Him. Not requesting anything, but affirming who I am in Him. God has given you a gift when He tells you to meditate. The knowledge of the Word of God helps you to understand who God is, but meditation let's you know HE IS REAL!

Joshua1:8 (NLT) "Study this Book of Instruction continually. MEDITATE on it day and night so you will be sure to obey everything written in it. Only then will you prosper and succeed in ALL you do." Meditation provides access to a special place where you can retreat and commune with God who is the Source of EVERYTHING. It is how you find yourself, an awesome person, a spirit being, a treasure to God. It's a place that changes you, you find forgiveness and love. It's a quiet place where you find freedom and peace. There is a treasure chest deep within you that God the Almighty has given you access to. Go there; take time and go, for your own sake!

God is a part of religion, but He is not bound to it. He has many attributes, many dimensions, and many faces. You serve a God who can do anything, yet is limited to how you think of Him at any particular moment in your life – that's who He becomes to you!

He meets us anywhere and everywhere. There is never a place He is not. If I go to heaven Lord you are there, if I make my bed in Hell you are still with me. God is there for you, no matter where you find yourself in life. On the mountain top or in the valley below...I can never escape from His presence. For He lives within me!

Who is God?

He is the wind that blows my hair as I walk through the valley of death, and grace in my time of need. He is my lover, friend and Father when I need intimacy and conversation. He is the rain that brings blessings to my life. The sun that warms my body, the ocean that steals my thoughts and the fragrance I smell in a flower. He is my first thought in the morning and my last thought at night. I see Him in everything and in everyone. Who is God? ***He is whatever I need Him to be at that moment!***

2 Peter 1:3 (NLT) "By His divine power, God has given us <u>EVERYTHING</u> we need for living a godly life. We have received all of this by coming to <u>KNOW</u> Him, the one who called us to Himself by means of His marvelous glory and excellence."

RELIGION VS SPIRITUALITY
"Something Must Be Broken"

"Religion is the means, not the end. It is the map, not the territory. It is the cover not the book." David Hawkins

Religion is seen in many different ways, by many different people:

To an outsider/unbeliever religion is its rules, traditions and doctrines. They also believe, religion asks for one mind, one belief system, and no flexibility. Praying at certain times, eating, abstaining from certain foods, studying from a specific text, learning certain songs or chants, restricted on what to wear or not wear, activities you may participate in or not and believing that's God's way of doing things. Not sure of who God is and not interested in finding out, because of the restrictions put on believers or followers.

To believers, religion becomes a place for social acceptance, a community, church family, a place for information gathering. It makes sure there is unity of thought and action in its members. It provides spiritual and physical support through the spoken and unspoken word, through teachings, outreach, leadership positions, traditions, doctrines and financial needs. Most religions have programs they have created, such as outreach, counseling, distribution of food and clothing to the needy outside and also within the church.

At times religions can unknowing produce self-righteous followers, full of judgment, strife, clicks, backbiting, division inside their communities, by creating an environment of separation; leaders from being accessible to members for whatever reason. The objective in servicing members becomes "What can they do for me and mine?" Some define their faith with boundaries that God never established. It's fruitless…the temple, the "church" is you! Not the place you gather on Sunday morning. ***I Corinthians 6:19 (NLT) "Don't you realize that your body is the temple of the Holy Spirit, who lives in you and was given to you by God? You do not belong to yourself."*** You are the church therefore you personally must understand who God is for you and operate accordingly. You take God with you wherever you go and your behavior should also demonstrate that. That is Spirituality, not religion!

Religion is a good foundation to an introduction to God, it is not God. You must develop a relationship with God as you would with any relationship after an introduction. Relationship is intimate, personal and needs an honest two-way conversation! Truth and God are found inside of you in silence, and it will be self-evident by your behavior. You will begin creating a better version of you, because you will understand who you are and who God is.

Religion asks you to learn from the experience of others. Spirituality encourages you to seek your own experiences. When you know Him then lives change because of it!

Religion encourages you to explore the thoughts of others and accept them as your own. Spirituality invites you to come up with your own conclusion from the God that lives with you. It shows you who God is and who you are in God than any religion. Who can be a better guide or teacher than the one who lives inside you and created you! He knows everything about you; now trust Him to guide your every step.

Most every religion originated with the foundation of spirituality and God. Religion started with God, then trickled down and began to lose its foundation and replaced with one's self-interest. Religion is a place you go if there is something you don't know or understand spiritual principals and God. It is not a place you go if you already know. Once you have found your path, know your way through life and understand that God is certainly within you and will lead and guide you, there is no need for gathering in a church especially if you are being taught the same thing you already know. ***"It is not enough for religious people to only be involved with prayer, rather they are morally obligated to contribute all they can to solving the world's problems." Dali Lama*** It's a time for you to continue your journey to where God leads without shame, condemnation or guilt. Jesus says, "He who the Son set free is free indeed." It's your responsibility to develop a personal relationship with God. You build disciples and let them go to their own communities as they live God in them, so they can touch those whom you cannot touch. Let them go and grow and touch other people lives with their life. That's how it is designed to work.

Religious groups are often created with their own agenda. It didn't start out that way, but because there is no accountability for their actions, you begin to substitute God for your leader. You came in search for God with walls you already created from situations and issues in your life. You find misinterpretation and a deviation from scripture focused on guilt, shame and sin which brings more condemnation and creates a greater separation from you and God, a wall that is hard to break through. You turned to religion to help you shattered the walls, not more walls to hide behind.

Religion has created a man-made God, in your image and likeness, your reasoning and your belief system. God is a part of religion, but He is not bound to religion. You kill the image of God with your thoughts, words and behavior. Like I said before, religion is a good foundation and introduction to who God is, but when you depend on others to interpret the Bible for you and take no responsibility to know God for yourself, you give them permission to lead you to wherever <u>their desired</u> end.

Religion is knowledge, information about who God is, and it begins your journey to spirituality. Faith and belief are necessary, but critical thinking (knowledge, asking questions when something doesn't sound or feel right in your spirit) it's necessary to complete it. Without a moral compass, looking within yourself for answers already there you will be led by blind faith…blind faith is just that BLIND! Too many have gotten a little truth and ran with it and destroyed lives, families, communities, and countries in the name of God! My purpose is not to remake you, but to let you know that Jesus restored you back to what God created you to be. You have been restored (back to your original form) not fixed. **Colossians 1:22 (NLT) "Yet NOW He has reconciled (restored) you to Himself through the death of Christ in His physical body. As a result, He has brought you into His own presence, and you ARE holy and blameless as you stand before Him WITHOUT a single fault."** My goal is to give you pause, another way to see you, something you may never have considered. To awaken the Spirit within you! God's truth!

True story, this happened June 2016 reported in the Sacramento Bee

A shooting at a gay bar in Orlando, Fl where 49 had been killed and many injured was such a tragedy, my heart went out to the families of those that died that day. However, my feelings were not shared by many Christians. Pastor Jimenez here in Sacramento began his Sunday morning sermon with "**I wish the government would line up all the gays and shot them. I was sad that the shooter didn't finish the job. It's our job to punish that behavior and it's not a tragedy when people who deserve to die, die!**" Let those words sink in for a moment. It was an all too familiar voice from many pulpits. These were individuals who died that day, their lifestyle had nothing to do with us loving them, praying for their families. How they live is between them and God. You are to live God so others may be saved. Spewing hatred from a pulpit to justify your behavior, thoughts or belief isn't what that pulpit is for. Jesus said love God, love your neighbor and watch your own life – judge yourself. **James 2:10 (NLT) "For the person who keeps all of the laws except ONE is as guilty as a person who has broken ALL of God's law."** It is only by God's grace you are where you are today. Someone prayed for you and loved you through your ugliness without judgment. It's time you begin to pay if forward. **Matthew 15:8-9 (NLT) "These people honor me with their lips, but their hearts are far from me. Their worship is a farce, for they teach man-made ideas as commands from God."** You ignore God's law and substitute your own TRADITIONS! You <u>**skillfully sidestep**</u> God's law in order to hold on to your OWN TRADITIONS!

You "skillfully sidestep" by giving rules that don't make sense and say God said, what to wear, how to wear it, what to eat or not eat, what to drink or not drink, what to watch or not watch, how to think or not think, how to enjoy life or not to enjoy life to all this you have labeled sin…

After my parents entered a different phase of their life… religion… I didn't realize the impact that would make on my life. It's one thing to look the same as those you attend church with; it's another to look different everywhere else. This really affects your self-esteem. I couldn't understand the obsession denominations had about making you look sooooo different than anyone else. They wear it as badge called 'HOLINESS." They are so interested on the outside appearance, but not as obsessed with healing the inside. What's really interesting each church you attend they all say they are Christians, but have different rules and doctrines. I was raised in the Apostolic Church…they called us "holy rollers." I was saved, bound to religion and still broken inside.

It was really hard for me as a Christian in school. I couldn't wear pants, shorts, short sleeve blouses or t-shirts. No cutting of my hair, no makeup, no jewelry, no dancing and no dating anyone that wasn't from the church. My dress or skirt had to be beneath my knees, I looked like Olive Oil in Popeye...long skirt, long sleeves and long socks the only thing showing was my knee caps. However my sister was clever, she showed me how to fit in a little with everyone at school, by rolling up my skirt. The problem with that is we walked around school always looking over our shoulder for our dad who would show up unannounced. With just that small infraction, which made me feel a little happier; I allowed guilt and shame to flood my mind because of it. I felt like Job, thinking that God was waiting for me to sin so He could punish me. **Job 10:13-14 (NLT) "Yet your real motive, your true intent was to watch me, and if I sinned you would not forgive my guilt." Job 9:14-16 "So who am I that I should try to answer God or even reason with Him? Even if I were right, I would have no defense. I could only plead for mercy. And even if I summoned Him and He responded, I'm not sure He would listen to me."** Job was not alone in his comments; I stood right there with him. Keeping the rules, regulations, doctrine I found I was serving God out of obligation...didn't want to go to HELL. Despising my life, despising God who created me, all because of religion!!! I had no relationship with God, never taught how to. My self-esteem, self-worth and self-confidence were 0%; all I felt was shame, guilt and condemnation. Self-esteem does not come from acquisitions and approval from others. Your body does better when your soul and spirit is healthy.

Pain comes from living others expectation of you and doing the same to others. When you have too many rules, and regulations your growth is limited, you must fail so you can understand and achieve success.

I was that person seeking validation from anywhere and

everywhere I could find it. Looking for acceptance wasn't available even in the church. The preachers would preach homeliness... excuse me holiness, but dated the ones that were the opposite of what they preached. I only wanted to be part of the group. I craved someone to tell me I was beautiful, good, and worth their time. I wanted so much to be loved and valued, someone to really know me, see me. I thought God was too far away to care. I never turned to Him for that, He was only good for answering my needs and punishing me. As I look back I think I lived my high school years with depression – didn't know it. I was suffocating inside with no place to go. I was confused; I was taught the non-Christian (which was any denomination that were not "Jesus Only.") was not available to date. Rules, doctrine, traditions, denomination, <u>NOT God</u> robbed me from my youth and most of my adult life. I was saved, and bound to religion.

However, God is so faithful even as I question His intent, His love, His motive, it never stopped Him from loving me and bringing people into my life that would guide me onto the right path which would show me how to know Him. Circumstances and people that were appointed to bring me to where I am today, free, whole and complete. People and books that taught me that it's vital to have intimacy with God and have a quiet place and time to be with Him alone!

We have truly forgotten the teachings of Christ. **"You have died with Christ, and He has <u>set you free</u> from the spiritual powers of this world. So why do you keep on following the rules of the world, such as, 'Don't handle! Don't taste! Don't touch!? Such rules are mere human teachings about things that deteriorate as we use them. These rules may seem wise because they require strong devotion, pious self-denial, and severe bodily discipline. But they have no help in conquering a person's evil desires." Colossians 2:20-23 (NLT)** Stop putting so much emphasis on the outward appearance and begin changing the inside spirit of a person. **"For the Kingdom of God** *is not a matter of what we eat or drink, but as living life of goodness and peace and joy in the Holy Spirit. If you serve Christ with this attitude, you will please God and others will approve of you too. So then let us aim for harmony in the church and try to build each other up." Romans 14:17-18 (NLT).* It becomes self-evident; the basis of who you are; which is a spiritual being having a human experience. You are not your body, it's only a vehicle for you to navigate through this world, you truly are a spiritual being, but you ignore the inside of who you are and focus on the outside. Looking for outside validation, outside approval instead of going within yourself to see that God approved of you, before anyone else ever got a chance to disapprove!

God has given you a tool called "discernment" whether you use it or not, it's present in every one of you. A simple way to know; there is joy when you hear the truth that can set you free, there's this feeling inside you can't explain but feels so awesome. The most powerful tool you have is experience, emotion, and you ignore this one the most. When you ignore it you experience things over and over. When you finally get it things change. At times you are told that God speaks only to "special people" and the rest of you are unworthy, not quite special enough. The problem is you remove your responsibility on how your life turns out and place it on the leader who has spoken into your life. You don't believe you must hear God on your own, and God is there waiting to have a conversation with you. But you have already decided that the "man or woman of God" have heard from God already, so you listen to them instead. By listening to what others say about God, you have decided you don't have to think at all.

Take control back for your own relationship with God, which is personal not to be given to someone else to do for you. You can't hear from God until you stop thinking you have already heard from Him through others. God doesn't reveal Himself outwardly, but through inward experience. You need to stop looking for answers outside yourselves, when the answer lies within…God!

Something Must Be Broken

Religion creates a "Let's make a deal" mentality, if you give me $$ whatever amount I'm asking for, God will take care of your need. But wait…if you don't heed to His calling, to His word you will not get your needs met. It's only if you give what I have instructed you to give. (Faith!!! I say this is faith in God's word). Who cares you don't have money for food, clothes, rent, you don't have because you won't give. You take many verses out that support that belief. You distort faith and prosperity for your own self-interest.

I sat under this teaching for years, and still hear these words spoken today. I was a single mom raising two children I would attend service and my finances weren't the best. I needed to pay bills and the preacher would finish his sermon saying that God said that there are three people here today that God says will give $100 and He will supply your need. I didn't have the $100 and so I left that service feeling defeated, unworthy, because God knew I didn't have it, so why would He offer that amount to supply the needs I had. I felt worse leaving then when I came in. I went to the church for help and they refuse to help me all they wanted was to pray with me. I didn't need prayer I needed money to help pay my bills. I had given all I had to the church, but didn't get what I needed, when I needed it. I always went back to thinking God was unhappy with me and my life. I blamed me for my situation and God was just punishing my missed steps. When you don't teach God's love and mercy, that His plans for you are good and not evil, you feel the way I felt. When you don't know that the Word of God says, bring whatever you have purposed in your heart and He would bless you, you feel defeated and unworthy. You question your life and decisions. I didn't know God. I didn't realize He literally lived in me and not up in heaven. He knew my desires, dreams, my thoughts and my needs. He really was a God of unconditional love and had great things in store for me. Sadly it took me a lifetime to learn!

Which brings me to those honorariums…God gave you His

Word to share with His people...it was a gift to you. He gave you revelation for those people without charge. It was a gift! Jesus paid the price for you. He never charged the people to hear Him speak. He taught the people for 3 ½ years, what would set them free and yet you have the nerve to quote scripture. "Give honor to where honor is due..." I'm not opposed to an honorarium, it's reasonable especially when you travel (hotel, transportation, food), I get it. However, there are singers, preachers, leaders charging $10,000 or more to minister for one or two hours, **"reasonable"** being the operative word. Paul who made it clear, that all was needed to give honor and respect to those that were spreading the gospel was to take care of their needs, not their greed!

"A preacher or minister is to be a live person, a real person, a true person and simple person. Who deals with the great truths of holy character and must impersonate those truths. There is power inherent in truth; but is often like electricity; needing a conductor to develop it. He who best commends the truth of the gospel to his hearers is he who has translated that truth into his own life."

"If you claim to be religious but don't control your tongue, you are fooling yourself and your religion is worthless. Pure and genuine religion in the sight of God the Father means caring for orphans, and widows in their distress and refusing to let the world corrupt you!" James 1:26-27 (NLT) Leaders have allowed the world to corrupt their perception on the purpose of religion. Some have manipulated their members by using phrases; "If you don't give, God won't answer your prayers." "Don't curse yourself by not giving to God." "If you want a miracle from God you must give of your finances...all that you have shows great commitment." They have built their million-dollar homes on religion, expensive cars, airplanes, churches in the name of God. While the widow, orphans, those in need go without in their own congregations and then have the nerve to say they are the way they are, because they lack faith. They have allowed the world

to corrupt them. They don't even call them churches; they are organizations, corporations, etc. Christ said, Go into the world and preach the gospel to everyone," not COME into my church and hear the gospel. You got it a little twisted.

Sowing and reaping affects every aspect of your life. The way you think, the way you speak the way you behave and what you believe not just giving of your finance. Much of what you do every day comes from habitual behavior over the course of time you have developed a way of approaching life. The human mind has a tremendous amount of power, as well as the spoken words. That which holds your attention determines your actions…What you think about all day long is what shows up in your life, that is the power of thought and actions! Where you are today is the result of the dormant thoughts in your mind. I can give all of my money and believe I'm not worthy of prosperity. I will only manifest what I believe and think … if I believe poverty and no self-worth, that is what I will manifest in my life. You don't have to necessarily change all of your thinking, just the few thoughts or belief systems that are keeping a positive attitude from flowing in you.

Here are the challenges in letting others interpret the Word for you:

You don't know what is the true message from God? Has the person's teaching come by way of meditation and pray, or has it come from other sources? The counseling session from the previous night, or their self-image about themselves, past or present issues become the main topic of that Sunday morning message Where and what motivation is that understanding coming from. The Word of God is powerfully all by itself. But you find yourself weeding out all the stories to find a Word from God. You are told to test it with your Spirit.

You don't only give the leader, teacher control of what you think, how you think, why you think, but you begin to believe what's important is the teacher not the teachings, you begin to idolize the leaders or worship them. If all you can hear is them and no one else. You don't listen to your spirit and exam those things that jump out at you; you just dismiss that feeling and continue to hear only them. Ask yourself these questions, 'How does your spirit feel about certain things you hear or see? Are you dismissing your intuition? You know those red flags that show up.

You are blindly following and obeying others without questions even when it makes no sense. God requires maturity in you. For you to come to Him so He can show you how you can grow in Him. This is a personal journey. You shall love God with all your heart, mind and soul, and there shall be no other god set before you. God says, I have other avenues that will help you to mature in Me and other experiences that will reveal who I am. Come to God along the path of your heart not through the journey of your mind. Your mind holds logic; your heart holds truth! God's way is not logical, it's spiritual. I am Spirit, you must come to me through the Spirit...it's a heart thing! **Proverbs 4:23 (NLT) "Guard your heart above all else, for it determines the course of your life."**

When the leader has sinned, what is your reaction, forgiveness or unforgiveness? Do you condemn them or understand they too can sin, and have God's mercy and forgiveness? Does it affect your walk with God? It's shouldn't, the leader is only a vessel that God has used to help you along your journey. **The "UN" in unconditional loves means "without judgment."** You are to love and pray for your leader, as for one another without judgment. That's true religion, so stop skillfully sidestepping God's word... LOVE INSPITE OF...

You are responsible for you! "Place no head above your own."

If you are told, you are the only true church and everyone else are unbelievers; you are encouraged to separate yourself from everyone else, isolate from the world. Jesus didn't say He was the true religion, He said, He was the Truth! He associated Himself with unbelievers. He said, "The healthy has no need of a physician, but those that are sick". How can you show the unbelievers who God is if you avoid them? God created everyone in His image and His likeness, God loves everyone the same. He is not a respecter of persons. The only difference between a believer and unbeliever is enlighten, knowledge of who God is. ***"If a person seems wicked, do not cast him away. Awaken him with your words, elevate him with your deeds, and repay his injury with kindness. Do not cast him away, cast away his wickedness."*** be different, be unique, God created you that way! The secret of your future is hidden in your daily routine. Don't conform to religion.

Conforming to religion changes you, because you become what others say you should be, and not what God created you to be. There are dangers in letting the physical drive you and not the spirit. You should check yourself, to make sure you are not ego base when it comes to your life. There are several ways to evaluated yourself and your true motivations for leading or living the life you are living. Are you separating yourself from those you teach (because you feel superior, more anointed of God), by assigning body guards to play interference for you.

Spirituality empowers, creates equality no difference between you and others. You can have those things God has promised to you, all you need to do is believe it, no conditions except BELIEVE. Spirituality says your worthy of God's promises. You have God within you to lead you and guide you literally. You are all that God said you are, and can be all that God said you can be, and have all that God said you can have. God loves you unconditionally, no condition to His love, because HE is LOVE!

Until you take time to learn who God is for yourself, you will continue to be frustrated, unfulfilled, and bound to religion, wearing it as a badge and judge those who won't agree with you. *"No man can be without his god. In the event that he has not the genuine God to favor and maintain him, he will have some false god to swindle and to sell him out. For each man has something in which he withdraws and resigns, he trusts and inclines toward. He fills up his thoughts in empty spaces of time, when he is alone, when he lies sleepless on his bed, when he is not pressed with other thoughts. Stuck in an unfortunate situation and distress toward the Creator; however, in the event that not on Him, then he leans on himself and others; rather than have no support at all. In the event that man does not wrap himself around God, he will find himself wrapped around something less desirable."* **Unknown**

You have the ability to hear from God, you can have your own desires manifested in your life. It's not a secret, what the leaders have; you have it too, just tap into the God that lives within you. Stop looking outside yourself for the answer look inside. Understand who He really IS for you! The promises are for you too! That means spending time with Him, and meditating on His Word; and waiting to hear from Him. He will give you His truth and His truth will set you free! You serve a God that loves you without conditions, look for Him everywhere, because He speaks through everything and everyone, you must believe it.

Life is nothing but experience for you to understand who you are. Jesus said, the things He has done, you can do also and greater things shall you do. THIS IS A POWERFUL STATEMENT! If you want to know what's true about something, look to how you feel about it, words will help you to understand, but experience allows you to know. It gives you clarity! Instructions are good, they tell you what to do, but you must experience it and use the instructions to help you along your path. God has given us instructions on how to know Him, now you need to live Him, experience Him, so you can truly know God. The problem with most people is they only read about God, but never experience

God. He speaks through many ways and if you can't see that you will always miss Him.

Experience is created in the invisible realm (faith) and manifested in your life. God becomes visible in miracles and every source of impulse of your life. You feel Him; you see His hand in your storms, trials, and troubles. Getting to know Him intimately, eliminates fear of everyday life and death, and can bring joy. Relationship is God and you meeting on common ground inside you. It's personal, intimate and real!

Experience is more important than instruction, or knowledge of a thing. If you read a book and it tells you how to swim, it doesn't mean you know how to swim, you just have the basic techniques, and in order to know how to swim you have to jump in the water and try the techniques you just read. You need to continue to jump in the water and trying to swim, once you have mastered it, experience it, you no longer need help with swimming. You can go by yourself and swim alone. It requires ACTION! EXPERIENCE! You can think about all day, but until you DO it, it will never happen. Job after his ordeal said, "I had only heard about you (referring to God), but NOW I have seen you with my own eyes." When you experience God for yourself, He becomes real. When you KNOW Him, you EXPERIENCE Him, and LIVE Him every day – This is spirituality, not religion. Faith without works is DEAD! Knowledge without experience is also DEAD! Street smart is more powerful than book smarts. It's all about <u>EXPERIENCE.</u>

Religion creates ownership of members when it's ego-base. It doesn't celebrate those they have invested in, encouraged and empowered as they move on to do the same. Instead they become offended when that particular person moves on to do the work of God without THEIR blessing. It's God that has given them their journey, their path not man. A way to evaluate that and make sure you are not conforming to religion or you're not operating in "ego-base" religion; is your Leader does what he says.

Spirituality has no interest in having control or power. Spirituality focuses on empowering men and women to become independent of that leader and dependent on God. Spirituality you become that which you believe God to be, because you have an intimate relationship with him. You don't need a title to know who you are.

Religion has it all wrong, they are trying to build great Cathedrals, and pack in stadiums for their own gain. They become the worshipped and the untouchable, the anointed one of God and everyone else is just ordinary people.

Spirituality says you can go to the throne of God boldly, you don't need anyone to go for you, you have the ability to speak to God and know Him for yourself. You have questions; He is there to answer them.

Religion creates titles that separate leaders from the people of God. When Paul said, "There are pastors, elders, teachers, prophets, etc." It wasn't a title to acquire; it was a behavior, a spiritual behavior. Stop chasing after favor or titles to display self-importance. When you chase after others approval, validation or opinion of you, be it good or bad you invite heartache and pain into your life. Learn to be independent of another person's thought about you. Look inside yourself and see God's perfection. If you seek outside approval then someone else's opinion or approval will be directing your life. Live by this statement "What others think of me is NONE OF MY BUSINESS!"

Spirituality is intangible, invisible, wordless, its experience not knowledge and the way you experience it is what Christ said, "When you pray go into your closet." You want to know God go into your quiet place and just think about Him without words and let God show you through experiencing His awesomeness, through His presence, who He is. Go within yourself and know He has always been there. You are not separate from God; you are always connected to Him. Put your ego, training, knowledge aside, open up your heart and mind and close your mouth and let God do the rest. You want true spirituality, true freedom within, that's how you experience it. Stop relying on others to tell you about Him, know Him for yourself.

Your body will literally change as a result of the shift in your belief system. You're bound to the thoughts you have about God, religion, spirituality, and truth. Everything you think you know is not necessarily the truth. Don't be surprised to find God may be the opposite of what you believe. Jesus said, "You shall know the truth and the truth WILL set you FREE." If you're not free, maybe you really don't know the truth yet. Jesus has left you a clear example of His truth, no interpretation needed. When you operate in doubt, not faith, you don't question God's ability, you merely doubt His desire. Even before you ask, I will give it to you which is God's promise to you.

How many are truly living an abundant life. Understanding God, He truly lives with you, not just saying it, but living it, experiencing Him. You have to understanding you serve an unconventional God; a God that is all thing to all people, not just the believers but the unbelievers. You preach Christ died for the sinner (world) so they will be saved. He did and they just haven't acknowledged Him yet. He died for EVERYONE! EVERYONE means EVERYONE!

Three things make up religion:

First it makes you lose confidence in yourself:

Secondly it makes you feel that it has the answers you don't:

Thirdly religion makes you acknowledge its answers without question.

Religion does not allow you to investigate the most basic – Who Am I? Where did I come from? Why do I exist (my purpose)?

Spirituality answers those questions when you understand your relationship with your Creator. Who Am I? I am a spirit being having a human experience. Where did I come from? From a Source (God) who was never born and will never die. Why do I exist, my Purpose? To create every moment of my life!

There is no mystery to life or a specific purpose. You just have a specific gifting that God has given you, a specific passion. Life is life and your purpose is to experience life. Your journey is made to lead you back to God and understand all that He is, you are! You are to make a better version of yourself each moment of each day. As you mature physically, you also mature spiritually. Open your heart and mind and let God lead you through the path He has set for you. When you let go and let God take you down your path, you find freedom, peace and relief. Literally go with the flow of life. Stop bucking the current, flow with it and you will always find peace and joy on the other side. You will be saved and free, not saved and broken, because you will know the Truth and it will truly make you FREE!

No journey is so far that the Spirit cannot lead you
No burden is so great that the Spirit cannot strengthen you
Without the Spirit the smallest obstacle
appears insurmountable

With the Spirit you are powerful and
unyielding diligent and determined
Capable of becoming all that you were created to be!

Mychal Wynn

LOVE - TRUE RELIGION

"It is not what he has, nor even what he does, which directly expresses the worth of a man, but what he is." – Henri-Frederic Amiel

Jesus said the greatest commandment that you can keep is "To love God with all your heart, love yourself and love your neighbor!" True love for God is to love everything and everyone God created. No conditions, no expectations, no demands, no favorites… just pure love!

LOVE GOD

I John 4:10 (NLT) "This is real love-not that we loved God, but that He loved us and sent His Son as a sacrifice to take away our sins."

Real love is God-driven, God-given, and God-empowered and originates from God. This gift is not from man to God, but God to man. God's love is in everyone and in everything. True Story this was in the Toronto Paper in 2003 *"A disturbed man, and potential mass murderer, had six thousand rounds of ammunition and multiple weapons. He intended to kill as many people as possible and then commit suicide. He could not be reasoned with; however, he was interrupted by a dog with a Frisbee who begged him to play. The would-be killer suddenly had a 'change of heart'* *he dropped the weapons, surrendered, and then sought help for his state of mind. The love of the dog (named Elvis) effortlessly accomplished the miraculous, which out any reasoning."* This story shows that God loves you so much He will use the extraordinary to save you; and the second it shows pure love can do the impossible. Your thinking restricts your ability to do the impossible, not your physical body. Everything to this point has been learned behavior even when it comes to loving. Because God literally lives inside you (ask Elvis) and He is the very breath that gives you life, there is nothing impossible for you. You already create every moment of your life by what you believe, what you think about love, money, sickness, relationship and everything else. Why not create your every moment aware…be intentional, take control of your life by taking control of your thoughts, your words and your action. If what you believe isn't bringing positive and peaceful change, maybe you need to rethink your belief system. In order to relearn about love with no conditions you'll need to know God who loves you unconditionally. Let's talk about God's love!

God's love leads to being complete, free and living a life of power. You say God my provider, Jesus my healer and He is all I need. You want to believe those words; however you look outside yourself to find those answers which are inward issues. God loves you, because of who God is, not because of anything you do or do not. He doesn't kick you to the curb, because you don't live the way others say you should or shouldn't. UNCONDITIONAL LOVE means just that, no conditions; it's too great a term to understand fully. You have determined God only answers prayer by how good you behave. If your definition of love is very conditional, love with no conditions becomes foreign. Foreign because you believe the lie that God cannot be trusted; His love cannot be depended upon; and that God's acceptance of us is conditional. If you cannot depend on God's love to always be there, then who can you depend on? If God will retreat and withdraw from you when you misbehave, or when you do not perform up to His standards, will not people too?

When Christians try to justify, debate or explain this small term "unconditional," it doesn't fit in their rules, church doctrine, or religion. If you can get a hold of that term and really understand what it really means, your life would be made free with all fullness of life and power that comes from God and you would stop kicking yourself every time you made a mistake or a bad decision. Just realize it was a mistake then decide to turn it around. It doesn't mean you're a bad person; it just means you probably should look within yourself and ask God to help you next time. Realize what God already knows; you are the most magnificent, most remarkable, and the most unique being He created! That's just how much He loves you! He does not love you because of your behavior. He loves you in spite of your behavior. He loves you because you are His child, and His creation. He said you are good regardless of what you think about you.

You must let go of the past and forge towards the future. Forgetting what hurt you, but never, never forgetting what it taught you; for pain is a necessary part of life, but suffering is not. You cannot be free while at the same time blaming others for your troubles. Blaming others takes an enormous amount of energy, which gives you a "drag-me-down" mindset that creates stress and disease. It makes you feel powerless over your own life. However, when you stop blaming others for your troubles you regain your sense of personal power. You must develop the desire to change that is the key to growth in all areas of your life. Remember what you THINK you become. When you let go of the past you can find yourself creating a better tomorrow. ***"The secret of change is to focus all of your energy not on fighting the old, but building the new." Socrates***

God lives within you. He can't get any closer than that. Look to Him when things come up that you need His assistance. He says simply ask, and I will answer; and He does. Just be open to unorthodox, unusual places to find it. It's not always where you think you will find it. Just open your heart, clear your mind and surrender to Him and let Him guide you to the answer, because He really does answer when you ask. He doesn't hold any good thing from you. You think your behavior keeps you from God answering when you need Him, it does not. His plans for you are good and not evil, to bring you to an expected end.

Love is a learned behavior – when you came into this world your mother, father, outside influences, teachers, friends and family told you what love was, not just told you but showed you. Everything that was taught, everything you experienced was conditional. You were told that they loved you only if you would comply with their expectations of you.

So because of those experiences as you grew up you learned to love with conditions. Your love for God, yourself and your neighbor also came with conditions. It becomes "What have you done for me lately?" You realized those that demonstrated their love for you was with conditions. They loved you until you didn't make them happy. They loved you until you misbehaved. They loved you until they didn't…conditions…conditions…conditions, and because of the conditions you internalized, misinterpreted love and began to blame yourself for their feelings about you. You began to have problems with self-esteem, self-worth and self-love. You looked outside for validation and value. You began to doubt your decisions and doubt God's love for you!

Many of the circumstances that blocked your progress in life were based on your assumptions you carried with you from what you have been taught. However, when you changed the way you looked at things, new pathways became available to you, new possibilities and opportunities showed up. ***"We cannot solve our problems with the same thinking that created them." Albert Einstein*** I was stuck on my assumptions, but God showed me many ways to deal with life without the pain and stress. I, not events, not circumstances, not even people give me the power to be free, happy and healed because God is not only beyond, but also deep within me.

God's word is created in your heart, that's where it starts. Then you speak and it's released in the atmosphere which gives God the ability to answer those things that you thought were impossible before He became real in you! What happens when you believe the impossible? Unusual blessings happen! **Mark 9:23 (NLT) "What do you mean, 'If I can?" Jesus asked. "Anything is possible if a person believes."** People that say they can and those that say they can't are both right. So if you believe God's love is conditional that is what you will experience, instead of knowing His love has no conditions.

If you would live this basic principal, you would open up a hold new realm in your life. If you would only practice these principals and I say practice because 90% of what you do is learned behavior. YOU have practiced religion so long; when Spirituality introduces itself to you, you're scared to accept it. Doubts arise because of an absence of surrender to the Spirit within. It is different then what is being taught and practiced, it's labeled "New Age." Anything that tells you to connect to the God within you is questioned. If you really understood who walked beside you, guided you on your path from within, you would never experience fear or doubt. **"Greater is He that is in me, then he that is in the world."** New Age...don't think so! Letting go of religion requires courage and faith. If you indeed want to know God, you will have to forget what you think you know and open up your heart and mind and He will show you the way.

"Be careful not to enter another's life if you cannot be a gift. Be a gift to everyone who enters your life and to everyone whose life you enter." Dr. Wayne Dyer

LOVE YOURSELF

Feeling imperfect has caused you to say everyone is full of imperfections. You think people in your life should act as you do, think as you think, be as you are. Politicians should have your values, your moral, and your belief system. You feel others should align with what you believe to be true and right, which you adopted from others around you; such as your parents, teachers, siblings, friends, and church leaders. You don't only judge others but you judge yourself. You have bought into what the church and world defines beauty, success, love, wealth, worth, value and the most important LOVE! So it gives you a false view of the way you see yourself and others.

"A humble person does not look down on others. He does not compare himself to others. He knows his self-worth."

Never allow other's opinion about you be more important than your own opinion of you. Know who you are and you will be free! You figured everyone has loved you with conditions. You think God loves you just the same, so you have not experienced freedom in loving another without conditions.

Look inside yourself and recognize yourself first as God's creation, which He Himself said, "You are good and perfect," so you will be able to see others the same way…perfect, complete, whole, and lacking NOTHING!

Self-love:

"The way you treat yourself sets the standard for others on how you demand to be treated. Don't settle for anything other than respect and self-love." Eckhart

If you seek outside approval then someone else's opinion or approval will be directing your life. The words that were used to describe you, your self-worth, self-image, and perceptions were developed by how your family treated you. Words are powerful and they are not easily forgotten. Your learned behavior, thoughts about yourself were created by the words of those closest to you, from there your self- image and self-love began to form itself. How they felt about you and how you were valued in their presences.

Then you take those ideas and values to many relationships, to work and to church. The thoughts about yourself is taken to every aspect of your life and gives you a false thought of God's love, because God must love you with those same values and conditions as everyone else does. You are looking for those things you do not have to fill an empty part of you. You compare yourself to other's success, achievements, trying to acquire validation from outside sources that really don't matter. You are in your mind first before you speak it in the atmosphere, and then it becomes so! Your mind is where the battle takes place.

You try to protect yourself with a false image of who everyone says you are, without a clue of who God says you are. You look outside yourself for value, validation, self-worth, self-love and strength. You say "I am invisible simply because people refused to see me." But in reality you have built up walls, you wear masks so they can't see you. You have made yourself invisible!

You cannot change what you refuse to acknowledge. If you're not free, if you're not living life without limits, full of joy and laughter, then you are bound! If you're holding onto the past, you can't go forward, you are bound. Forget those negative thoughts; ideas that others are speaking into your life. You control your destiny, your self-worth, self-image and self-love…it starts with you (self). Right now, you are living others-image, others-love, others-worth of you.

If you don't have love for yourself, you do not trust the God that created you. God is love and you were created as He is "LOVE". You came from God who determined the color of your eyes, hair and the shape of your body. You came from a God that wished for you to succeed in whatever you choose to be. He desires for you to prosper as your soul prospers. King David said it best in Psalms 139: 13-18 (NLT) *"You made all the delicate, inner parts of my body and knit me together in my mother's womb. Thank you for making me so wonderfully complex! Your workmanship is marvelous, how well I know it. You watched me as I was being formed in utter seclusion, as I was woven together in the dark of the womb. You saw me before I was born. Every day of my life was recorded in your book. Every moment was laid out before a single day had passed. How precious are your thoughts about me, O God. They cannot be numbered! I can't even count them; they outnumber the grains of sand! And when I wake up YOU ARE STILL WITH ME!"* It all begins with your thoughts about you, let go of the labels others have placed on you. Give yourself permission to be perfect, even with all of your imperfections.

Fear:

"Our life is what our thoughts make it!" **Marcus Aurelius**

Fear is a strong emotion that holds you bound and does not come from God. **2 Timothy 1:7 (NLT) For God has not given us the spirit of FEAR; but of power, and of love and a sound mind."** So, where does it come from? It comes from others opinion of you, who you should be, trying to live up to those unrealistic expectations. It comes from the world system which creates fear base ideas and belief systems. Every action taken is based on love or fear, and not only in relationships, but also in every aspect of your life. Many of what you desire to do, every thought, every action is based either in fear or love. Every free choice you ever taken arises out of one of the only two possible thoughts; a thought of fear or a thought of love. Fear comes from you and you seem powerless to change the way you offer love to another, because that's all you know. What your inner self says to you – your deficiencies, your abilities, and your self-worth. Fear comes when you feel overwhelmed by the unknown. Fear is the spirit which contracts, closes down, draws in, runs, hides, and kills your dreams. Fear wraps your body in clothing, clings to and clutches all that you have; fear holds tightly to your emotions.

"Fear is only as deep as the mind allows"

Operating in fear kills your dreams, desires, passions and abilities and paralyzes you from moving forward. It creates unnecessary stress, false belief and stops you from being the entire person God created you to be, to have and to do. Complete, nothing missing and nothing broken! Fear makes situation appear bigger than what they are, step out in faith and leave your fear behind! The best thing about the future is that it comes one day at a time. God has given us the Spirit love. Love is a spirit which expands, opens up, sends out, stays, reveals, shares and heals. Love allows you to stand naked without shame, and gives all that you have away. Fear and Faith have only one thing in common… the unknown. Fear holds you, keeps you bound. Faith gives you the treasures you seek because you are in motion.

"The cave you fear to enter holds the treasures you seek." – Joseph Campbell

There are two laws that God put in place, and these laws never change. You can be, do and have whatever you can think or imagine; and you will always attract what you fear. Your emotions are so powerful they attract that which you fear the most, because your emotion is energy in motion. If you desire to be FREE, get rid of fear. Throw away negative thoughts out of your head. Release all doubts. Reject all fear. You want to have POWER, get rid of fear. You want to have wisdom, and a sound mind to make healthy decisions, get rid of fear. You want to Love yourself as God loves you, get rid of fear. Renew your mind. Retrain your mind. Be conscious of what you are thinking. You own and control that; you can't give that responsibility to anyone else. You must be word conscience, deliberate, and aware. Words are important and powerful, they are like little seeds that produce after its kind. Take care of your thoughts when you are alone, and take care of your words when you are with people!

Forgiveness:

"Forgiveness is the fragrance that the violet sheds on the heel that has crushed it." Mark Twain

The best gift to give to your enemy is FORGIVENESS! Un-forgiveness robs and blinds you from your purpose and destiny. God created you with greatness, power, passion, destiny, clarity and vision. When you can't or choose not to, you place a veil over your spiritual eyes. You become blind to God's love, because all you see is injustice…poor me…no one cares what they did to me… you no longer are a victim, but you can't see anything else. Un-forgiveness is the root problem to anger, pain, rage, no self-worth, no self-love, and no self-esteem. Cut off the root of un-forgiveness and the scales that blind your spiritual eyes will fall off. The truth is you don't have the power to change the past, but you have the power to live at this present moment the way you choose. Forgiving doesn't take away the memories, but it will take away the pain. So let go of those things that you cannot change. You have given those things enough wasted time in your life. *"Many are the affliction of the righteous but the Lord shall deliver me from them all."*

"Put on your new nature, created to be LIKE God, truly righteous and holy." Ephesians 4:24 (NLT) You were created to be like God. It's His Spirit that gives life to you. Return to what you came from LOVE – GOD! I say I am of God, I am God's essence and I need no human to confirm it. I trust who I am and I act on this perspective. I stay with the Truth and not what is false. *"So stop telling lies. Let us tell our neighbors the truth, for we are ALL part of the same body." Ephesians 4:25* Be like God,

live God, act without a sense of self. Give without conditions, see without preference.

Jesus represents the God of Truth, mercy and forgiveness. The Bible says in so many words, that the God of revenge was replaced by the God of mercy, grace, love and forgiveness. When God says to love your enemies, pray for them and not take revenge on them that is for your benefit, for your healing, and that is the only way you can live FREE! Be thankful for the experiences of your past, and begin to create new and positive memories. It's time for you to begin healthy relationships; because love is **forgiving** and love is **for giving**!

Today I pledge to be the best possible me,
no matter how good I am, I know that I can become better

Today I pledge to reach for new goals, new challenges,
and new horizons

Today I pledge to listen to the beat of my drummer,
who leads me onward in search of dreams

TODAY I PLEDGE TO BELIEVE IN ME!

Mychal Wynn

LOVE YOUR NEIGHBOR/ENEMIES:

There is no point in hating one's enemies as they will bring themselves down of their own nature".

If you neglect your love to your neighbor, in vain you profess your love of God. Loving your neighbor is how you demonstrate your love for God. Loving is not a thought but a behavior. It is who you are!"

What does it mean your Neighbor... it is everybody who you interact with; your family, friends, and strangers. It is the persons who live in your neighborhood, in your town, and in your congregation or church family, true love begins here. To love and be kind to your neighbor is the absolute starting point of genuine religion. **James 1:27 (NLT) *"Pure and genuine religion in the sight of God the Father means caring for orphans, and widows in their distress and refusing to let the world corrupt you."*** But beside these, it is also everyone who comes across your path, whoever it is, and who you have any method for helping – the troubled stranger you meet in traveling, the abused person who nobody has taken the time to care for. The homeless person that you pretend you don't see and are quick to judge, this too is your neighbor.

You don't know enough about your neighbor's past history or present situations to judge or condemn them. Just as your neighbors know nothing about YOU and YOUR issues! Jesus says in Luke 7:24 "Look beneath the surface so you can judge correctly." See beyond the behavior, walk in their shoes "see them" then if you wish you can judge them. But remember the same harshness you judge them, you too will be judged.

Too often we underestimate the power of a touch, a smile, a kind word, a listening ear, an honest compliment, or the smallest act of caring, all of which have the potential to turn a life around.

People come into our lives for a reason, a season, or a lifetime. Embrace all equally!

Love your neighbor, and you demonstrate your love for God. If your love has some other thought process, hidden agenda, manipulation, and another interpretation, it is false love and false self-esteem. For in God's eyes everyone is equal and loved with no conditions and in turn, you too are to love that way.

Therefore, what God has asked you to do is possible. When you exercise the Spirit side of you, everything else becomes easy. Love goes beyond boundaries, beyond racial lines, beyond religious differences, beyond anything that causes hate or conflict to reside. Love is POWER and God's love lives in ALL of us. Let us begin to live God, not just talk God! Nothing will change unless you change.

Keep your thoughts positive because
Your thoughts become your words.

Keep your words positive because
Your words become your behavior.

Keep your behavior positive because
Your behaviors become your habits.

Keep your habits positive because
Your habits become your values.

Keep your values positive because
Your values become your destiny.

-Mahatma Gandhi

PRESSED BEYOND MEASURE

"Impossible is just a big word thrown around by small men, who find it easier to live in the world they've been given, than to explore the power they have to change it. Impossible is not a declaration, it's a dare. Impossible is potential. Impossible is temporary. IMPOSSIBLE IS NOTHING!"

There are many types of pressures in this world: Atmosphere pressure, blood pressure, pressure groups, pressure gauge, static pressure, peer pressure, etc.

Webster defines pressure as "the burden of physical or mental distress"; an effect which occurs when force is applied on a surface; the constraint of circumstances, the weight of social or economic imposition.

Take a moment right now and think about the word pressure... we have all experienced pressure in one form or another, and some may be in the midst of it as we speak. The word pressure is like a word picture, you really don't have to say anything more about it. When someone says they are pressed beyond measure, you know what that is, you feel it, experience just by the word itself.

The best pressure that I can relate to is atmosphere pressure, when it builds up, you see and experience a storm. You know how big the storm will be by how the storms form. The bigger the pressure the more dangerous the storm.

You usually watch the news to see how strong the storm will be – you watch the trees as they move with the wind, how hard the rain is falling, if there is thunder and lighting and hail coming down. You stay informed of how big this storm will be. Once you have an idea about it, you begin to prepare for it. You get supplies, or you need to evacuate you hope your home will be there when you return. You take those things that are the most important to you. Some stay where they are and ride it out. They have their supplies, candles, water, can goods, shutters for their windows, etc.

There are floods, flash floods, hurricanes, tornadoes and degrees are given to each one depending on what they see in the system. Sometimes you have a chance to prepare other times you don't'.

On the west coast we experience earthquakes once and awhile, they too erupt because of pressure on the fault. The bigger the pressure the dangerous it is. The bigger the number the more destruction it brings.

People that are accustomed to hurricanes and tornados prepare their homes to sustain them. Some have shelters built, others stock their basements so when they show up they are safe from them. They see the problem and prepare for it., they safeguard their homes.

"Your actions today, define your future tomorrows." Watch what you're doing today – with your thoughts, your words and your actions.

If you can see the warning signs of storms, hurricanes, tornados, and earthquakes, why do you ignore the warning signs when your body and spirit give you, when pressure is beginning to build up inside of you. Your body talks to you all the time. You ignore it and soon the warning signs become more intense and more dangerous. Your behavior is only a symptom of a problem you refuse to address, you avoid it like the plaque, and find yourself in the midst of a storm, pressed beyond measure! You need to safeguard your heart...safeguard your life. Paul makes it clear in Corinthians.

*2 Corinthians 1:6-10 (NLT) "Even when we are **weighed down with troubles**, it is for your comfort and salvation! For when we ourselves are comforted, we will certainly comfort you. Then you can patiently endure the same things we suffer. (7) We are confident that as you share in our sufferings, you will also share in the comfort God gives us. (8) We think you ought to know, dear brother and sisters about the trouble we went through in the province of Asia. We were **crushed** and **overwhelmed** (pressed beyond measure) beyond **our ability** to **endure** and we thought we would never live through it. (9) In fact, we **expected to die**! But as a result, we **stopped relying** on **ourselves** and **learned** to rely **only** on God, who raises the dead. (10) And He did rescue us from mortal danger, and **HE WILL** rescue us again. We have placed our confidence in Him, and **HE WILL** continue to rescue us."*

Paul is saying when your pressed down, others are watching to see how you will react to your storm, your pressure. He says, pressed beyond measure...do you see that...pressed BEYOND measure. You feel flat as a pancake, you have so much pressure you feel your head will explode. He says it's for your salvation... Has Paul lost his mind...How can being pressed beyond measure be for my salvation? Well Paul is not alone in his assessment, James had the same idea in James 1:3.

James talks about embrace, and face it with joy, your trials, tribulations, troubles because it challenges your belief system (salvation), it shows what's inside you...what you are really made of…and it just doesn't' show you it tells you to WORK IT OUT… look to God to help you, heal you, so you can be complete, lacking NOTHING!!! STORMS ARE FOR YOUR OWN SALVATION!!! They are potential teachers to save you from YOU, the student.

Stop being so proud to share your troubles, to relieve the pressure by sharing it with someone you trust, learning to give it to God and allowing Him to bring the right people into your space, your life so you don't allow the pressure to build up inside you. You are not an island alone, refusing to share your troubles, your depression, your pressures with anyone because you think they will judge you, question your faith or your love for God. Feeling sorry for yourself, playing the victim and the blame game doesn't help you overcome. Allowing fear to drive you, only delays your victory, your peace, your change and your healing. Allow God to help you in your time of trouble. Let Him guide you along your journey, along your storm, so when healing occurs, you may have saved a life without knowing it. Sharing becomes salvation for you and others. Paul said he shared his troubles so OTHERS can learn from him. Your victory can be someone's salvation.

God wants you to know He understands – He sees you, not how you see you, how you see your storms, your pressures, your troubles, but He sees your heart, your soul, your power. He sees Himself in you and says I do understand, now understand this… take the power I've given you and change you! For you are the sums of your thoughts. Problems come in many shapes, sizes and degrees of seriousness that you wish never happened. One moment you feel on top of the world, suddenly the world is on top of you. When something doesn't meet with your approval, you operate in assumptions. When in doubt it must be someone else's fault. When you think like this you don't take responsibility for your own actions, problems, anger, frustrations, depression, stress and unhappiness. For whatever is missing in your life, is something you do not value. Value yourself, value love, value forgiveness, value self-worth and that will be a part of you.

Something Must Be Broken

There is a benefit in your storms, in your troubles, in your trials; it brings you to your knees. It causes you to seek the face of God; because all you want is answer from Him. You cry out to Him, not realizing that's all you need, to open the door to the "presence of God."!

I was in the midst of one of my storms. I was pressed beyond measure, my back against the wall, no place to go. I wanted to believe what I was going through was for my good, but I couldn't see through my pain, my past, my insecurities, my doubt, my heart issues and my problems seemed too big to handle I didn't know how to be free from the same old troubles. It just crept up inside me. Things that I had buried, found its way back to the surface. I was saved, but still broken and it always took a storm that brought it back up. I refused to acknowledge it and tried to bury it. I felt hopeless, depressed, alone, over taken by fear and sick inside. No answers, no faith! No one knew the struggles, no one knew the troubles, and no one knew I wanted to die. I was tired of the struggles and in the midnight hour, when the house was quiet, everyone asleep I went downstairs and did what **Abraham Lincoln** *said he does in times like these* **"I have been driven many times upon my knees by the overwhelming conviction that I had nowhere else to go. My own wisdom and that of others seemed insufficient for that day,"** *Others man made wisdom or opinions didn't help. Telling me it would be alright, didn't help either. Nothing I thought I knew to make it through did not help me. With tears streaming down my face, feeling overwhelmed and scared I cried out to God… Run your fingers through my soul. For once, feel exactly what I feel. I NEED YOU!!!*

And God said. "Look inside yourself and find that I have always been through the abuse, pain and brokenness, I experienced it with you, NOW let me heal you so you can have an intimate relationship with me. So you can know me for yourself and know that I HAVE ALWAYS LOVED YOU!"

It's amazing when you're pressed the thoughts that come across your mind, you forget all the religious teachings, and you just want the pain to go away anyway you can. Thank God that He doesn't think as I think, because He was there all the time and He came through for me. He showed up and showed out! I am so grateful for it, because when trouble came my way again, I knew God was there to guide me through it. I realized that my struggle was new to me, but not God, He saw it long before it showed up in my life. So I had to believe that it came for my good, my maturity; to challenge my belief system and my walk with Him. Was I living the Word or just hearing it!

Storms shake your insides; make you evaluate your belief system, yourself worth, your relationship with God! It's hard to know God, have a relationship with Him when there is a wall between you! Storms come to challenge your faith and to destroy your walls.

There are times you create your own pressures by trying to impress or keep up with the "Jones." Thinking that's how you will be accepted, respected and valued. Be aware of your snowball effect from your thinking. Looking for outside approval, outside validation to the point you're drowning in debit and you're walking around saying "God has blessed me with this house, this car, this and that." Drowning.... depressed...stressed...pressure...back against the wall... **Proverbs 10:22 (NLT) "The blessings of the Lord enriches and He adds no sorrow to it."**

Sometimes when storms hit, your force to evacuate, leaving everything behind to save yourself. Storms come into your life for you to let things go. Holding onto past stuff, present issues and pressures can KILL YOU! It's weighing you down. You feel you have nowhere to go. The pain – the issues of the heart – un-forgiveness is killing your spirit and bringing physical sickness to your body...EVACUATE... Let go and let God jump start your spirit. Let go of other people's opinion, validation, your thought and judgments. However letting go doesn't make sense to you, because you just don't understand God's way of deliverance. ***"In the middle of every difficulty lies opportunity." - Einstein***

You must mature spiritually and see trials, troubles as a growing tool that is helping you through life. God's way is not our way. He says trust the process regardless of what your natural eyes sees, what this natural world says, because I alone see the whole picture, I know the finish product.

Pressure determines how big your storm will be, it doesn't just teach you to see yourself correctly, but also to see God correctly, your vision is readjusted, your priorities change, your pursuit for God intensives and you eventually evaluate and examine yourself to find the truth of your troubles. The greatest promise that Jesus gave you was not that you would not have tribulations, <u>but you can overcome them.</u> There is a divine purpose behind everything and therefore a divine presence in everything. God is life, He is the stuff life is made from. Nothing exists – nothing- without a reason understood and approved by God.

I'm convinced today that my dad must have been sick and tired of being sick and tired of his life, of his behavior, of his pain when he came into that church. I believe now he must have cried out to God previously before he walked into that church. But I'm pretty sure he did not expect to get the answer the way it came. He came for a different reason, but God was waiting for him and the help he asked for came and it came unexpectedly and suddenly.

Storms/pressures will definitely bring you to the arms of God, especially when you're at the end of your rope. Sadly that's what it takes at times. You have to be sick and tired of being sick and tired before you will allow God to bring the greatness out of you. Trust God and Love Him with all of your mind, body and soul. Be happy in knowing God! ***"Be sure you put your feet in the right place, then stand firm." - Lincoln***

You say you're the essence of God; you cannot be God like without pressure - without storms – without trouble –without trials. You never know how strong you are, until being strong is the only choice left for you. It's a necessary process in order to extract the best of what you have to offer. Olives must be pressed to their limits before you can enjoy olive oil which has so many different uses. But olive oil could not work without the olive! It doesn't matter how you press the olive, if you use a slug hammer, squeezer or juicer as long as olive oil comes out.

You choose what you do with your storms, and your pressure. How you choose to go through it, will either save someone or challenge your belief system. Storms become like ice you can resist it and keep slipping into a posture of defeat, or embrace it and glide through it with peace and resolve. When you're pressed beyond measure it can transform your life. It works out those attributes that are not like God, it uncovers your true nature. It's a mirror looking back at you, telling you there is something that needs to be worked out, overcome and let go of.

Build up your relationship with God, hold onto Him in your time of struggles…He hasn't changed…He still carries your burdens…He still gives you grace in your time of need…He loves you with no conditions even when you want to whine, complain and blame Him for your situations…He lets you know you're not alone. He says, "He is with you always until the end of the earth."

"Calm mind brings inner strength and self-confidence, so that's very important for good health." - Lama

SCRIPTURES USED FOR EACH CHAPTER

PRELUDE: Luke 10:33-37

PERSONAL TRUTH: Proverbs 4:23, Proverbs 5:21-23, 1 Timothy 4:4

WHO IS GOD: Colossians 1:15, Genesis 18:1, Joshua 1:8, 2 Peter 1:3

RELIGION VS SPIRITUALITY: 1 Corinthians 6:19, Colossians 1:22, James 2:10, Matthew 15:8-9. Job 10:13-14, Job 9:14-16, Colossians 2:20-23, Romans 14:17-18, James1:26-27, Proverbs 4:23

LOVE: James 1:27, 1 John 4:10, Mark 9:23, Psalms 139:13-18, 2 Timothy 1:7, Ephesians 4:24-25

PRESS BEYOND MEASURE: 2 Corinthians 1:6-10, Proverbs 10:22

SELF – EVALUATION

1. What is your truth?

2. Is religion the same as spirituality? Why?

3. What do you believe, and how does it affective your life?

4. Do you believe God answers your prayers in spite of your behavior? Does He love you without conditions?

5. Are you living a peaceful, loving, and free life or are you faking it until you make it?

6. What does God see that no one else sees, what does He know that no one else knows about you?

7. When you visit church, temple, mosque, cathedral, is it out of obligation or love?

8. How do you treat unbelievers or those that don't believe the way you believe?

9. How do you really feel about your life? Are you always seeking approval from others around you?

10. What we love is the foundation of our happiness, what is your foundation and does it bring joy to you?

11. Do you allow others to define who God is to you?

12. Are you allowing your past to define your future?

13. Who is God to you?

14. How do you feel about your relationship with God?

15. What are you more religious or spiritual, or do you see any difference?

16. When you are pressed beyond measure, what comes out of you?

17. When you operate in stress, has does it manifested in your life?

18. What mask have you been wearing or discarded lately?

19. What do you think about prosperity? Why?

CPSIA information can be obtained
at www.ICGtesting.com
Printed in the USA
LVHW042343121020
668648LV00003B/218